Norman Allan

as the Universe

selected poems

Just Testing

Contents

I am planning to dedicate

Norman Allan as the Universe

to

Brenda

but

Just Testing

is for

Miguel

whose voice is this

it's funny
       who speaks
the cockney boy's not me
       it's a memory of my teens
tithing my tongue
       to a person
and it's not me

i'm american ashkenazi
ash can nazi   my good lord
a mortal enemy a nemesis
branded into?onto our name

and i'm tripping down some
freudian and paranoid
satanically insignificant
red herring

it's funny
       who speaks
it's never
       quite me

whose voice is this

Twilight

Twilight sighs
reaching back towards our beginnings.

The night wind breathes a hush
upon our brow.

The sun lies now
behind our dreams:
our winnings
and our losings
balance in the seed
from which the future grows.

It is the bewitching hour.

Wish upon it.

the thing is

(I was puzzled that in my room,
where I am surrounded
with Buddhas and Hindu gods,
there is no Jesus…
I whirled around
and settled down
and realized …)

the thing is
you don't bow down to Jesus
you just open your heart
and say
love is an option

you don't bow down to love
you don't bow down to love
you open your heart

love is an option
love is an option
love is an option
just open your heart

Consider the Lilies

she said we come from the light
but I say we are molded from mud
and that explains all our stupidities

we're pretty smart for beasts
but locusts perish
in rat city it's dog eat dog
and whether we wake or not
matters only a jot
cause it's all already accomplished

God is evolved
mud into mind
mind into spirit
worlds without end

we are vouched safe in a flower

Untitled: I don't see...

I don't see that the Creator is evident in His creation. I think, for the
most part, this "miraculous" world once uttered in the Big Bang
unfolds through quantum and Darwin. For the most part
the Creator hides
as men spin lies
and the devil rides
in our hearts
along with the worriers and the warriors
and the glad-eyed boys
dancing dancing
with the kiss-me girls
so wanting to trust love

the Creator hides
in the dolmen arch
hides in the graves
and the grass
blades of Blake and Solomon
and in the tears of so many virgins

the Creator hides from our reproach
hides from our blush
hides in the open
a burning bush
in the mind

Untitled: this side of Atlantis

This side of Atlantis
we put on flesh,
fleshed out the ego
we so proudly wore
lighting the sky,
loud as God.
Lucifer was a myth,
a dream.
He didn't exist
in our great scheme,
unless he was in all of us.
How surprised we were
when the walls fell down.
From the rubble of Atlantis we built.

The Swastika

Oh see the bright-starred iron wheel
my history my industry
the threshing floor
poor chaff poor wheat
the spillage seeps
while trees grow metal wings
fly skyward blue fire belching
dreams the stars the heavens revolving
spitting sparks and crazy webbing

have you bound my people?
Moloch! Mammon!
tied them backwards
Auschwitz, Hemel Hempstead
poor chaff poor wheat
the spillage seeps
red
and brown

Nimrod is building in glory…

I read that to Murray Corngold
who sez what's that all about
I sez the swastika
he sez how so
I sez

Elijah lay down and saw the sky revolve,
the firmament swirling, seraph rounding God,
the feathered radiance of sphere within sphere
and six-fold wings beating over him, fa fa far,
the soaring hub and universal fire,
centre, energy:
this the ancient Vedics glyphed
卐 the swastika
But the goblin kingdoms
built a working model of this god
it burnt the fields

Now we build in chrome-titanium-plasma-fire.
Now it hums
Before the war they built in tin and steel.
Back then they worshipped
the internal combustion engine,
flywheels singing
heat-exchange gruyere-sleeved exhausts,
exhausts, stuttering exhausts, retorts,
stuttering wheel of fire:
the goblin's precious child

Oh see the bright-starred iron wheel
my history my industry
the threshing floor
poor chaff poor wheat
the spillage seeps
while trees grow metal wings
fly skyward blue fire belching
dreams the stars the heavens revolving

have you bound my people?
Mammon! Moloch!
tied them backwards
Hemel Hempstead, Auschwitz
poor chaff poor wheat
the spillage seeps
red
and brown

Nimrod is building in glory:
see! he raises his brow
and threads his bow

I Am His Own Devil

I am his own devil
who skews his eyes
and covets the purse
and the pussy
who stifles delight

I am his curse
his I'll be damned
I sour the milk
of all my achievements
piss off

I'm just mean
spike you for spite
spit in the face
of all your longings

I scorn to be soft
I grab for
with fist
to be first
take what's before me

I'm Lord of the Manor
or some angry madman
in gutter cursing
fuck you arsehole
I'm better

My Problem

my problem is I'm negative
the world though is horrible
and lovely
is lovely and horrible
that's my problem

my problem is I'm irritable
that's my problem
there's irritable weather
on my schoolyard door
cobbled streets I've stood on
with a hungry belly

learning to cope with appetite
watching it strangle and rape
little Sharon Morningside
and worrying that worrying
is part of my problem

I come down on poisons
that's my problem
I don't know where I'm going
but I'd like to see Jerusalem
without police

Jesus has angels who avenge with fire
that's our problem

Reincarnation

In my last incarnation
I was a bleating sheep
I followed the sunshine gladly

I remember the journey to slaughter
stock car stockyard
electric prod and stun gun
all your humanity

Ba ba black
ain't coming back
waiting your curse
your knife
my life

Now I'm lamb chops

for Rosamunda

if we didn't hold on to our pain
we would be like angels
we would fly away

but I've cherished the dross
clung to my sadness
so not to betray
the sulky boy
who won't forgive the petty things
the lack love
and the little disappointments

I am a snake consuming myself

where the fox gnaws its leg
to escape the trap
I've scratched my wounds
to remain in a finite regression

the landscape recedes
a mobius strip
through oblivion's womb

and if I wasn't so stuck
up my own ass
I'd be an angel
I'd fly away

Roots, the poem (explained)

I found myself in a nostalgic mood
thinking of a lost love
so "listless and bored"
I wrote of "toasting the hoard
the faces that filled my life and vanished"
then I waxed dramatic spouting how
I'd "striven with grief and twists
and briefed my soul to reach
for simplicity and splendour
to search and set high goals
and leave them high
for the wind to bless"

I thought again of "the joy of seeing
some dear face"
of "the fastness lent
by love reflected
these things that tied me to the world
anchors roots
these things that gave me substance
meaning"

so I arrived at these lines
how "I grieve to leave
this marrying web
stepping once more
through the open door
not turning my head
as did Lot's wife to salt
but standing beyond the doorways
which close forever on forever
standing as Jesus walked on water
before 'I don't know'
and 'I might never see your face again
my mother father lover friends'

scattered spider thread"

For Seth

Tony Blair culled a million cows,
a million sheep.
They blackened the skies.
Seth said he nearly became a vegetarian,
and he said he realized
that everybody is just doing the best they can.
"Tony Blair gets up in the morning
and does the next most important thing."
"As did Hitler," I said.
"Yes, as did Hitler."

Of course, one of the big questions is why aren't we holding fast
to our childhood dreams? Why aren't we living up to our potential?
Seth says it's easier to take a whinge.

"Yeah," I said. "Sometimes needs gnaw and wants want a bushel;
a roll in the hay every day, a different lass, a looking glass
to see myself augmented. I want a tiara and I want applause.
I want appreciation and not to care if I repeat myself,
or spout ardent nonsense.

Like Tony with his million sheep,
or Hitler with his Jews,
I want to know I've done my best,
and you to know it too."

Debby says

I don't want or need
the world to understand me

desolation is my best friend
there I feel profound

ecstasy is a barren moonscape

I listen to the silence
whispering my name

Debby says
she stands alone
but she's chasing her reflection
over the moon

he
her singular friend
he's not coming home
he's not coming home

alone
at the edge of the world
the night wind whispers
desolation
desolation

is there a word for the absence of resonance?

all these lines don't meet

the dog in the park
he's a stranger

decades of effort
to get back here
a wasted journey
the water's flowing
and you are nothing but a stranger
a dream

i pick up the pieces
put them away
and hope that you'll be there
another day

there is no reason
in this embedded universe
no reason
just rhyme

is "irresonance" a word?
is "irresonance" a word?
is "irresonance" a word?
is "irresonance" a word?

possibly 32nd St. in September

the small space
between your life and mine
is full with all the world
and all of time
all the TV channels' blare
can't break the silence

the night is between us
the days stand in our way
rivers of time

a few evenings ago
as I sat in the garden contemplating the space
between two knots in the wooden fence
I realized that bliss is accessible
just there
just grab it

and then what?
then hewing wood and carrying water
the falling towers
and Georgie's New War.

the small space between us
is a river of time
and all the world's a Jumping Jack
waving from oblivion
to our separate soul illusion

down on 32nd Street
the mundane flows on forever
papa's got a brand new bag
and Shakespeare's in the alley
the space between us seeks resolution
the On-Going Cosmic Rut
fills all space and time

I'm in the garden talking to the spiders
and all the channels blare

Music as Buddhogen

Ee's as complex as any of us
but he spends his days
his life playing music
which lends him some bliss
cause it spills him into wordlessness
highlights flux (the mirror of impermanence)
and makes emptiness easy
music: the void that dances
selflessly

Ezra talks of suffering

Ezra said
where the vulnerable reveals itself
we feel our pain
sharing turns our pain to love

look into the depth of your pain
into it's endless beauty
In the deep recess of the heart
love sleeps

We are like fountains
The power of pain
is to roll the stone
from the well of love
the spring of giving

No no no said Ez
The pain strips you bare
brings you to a meaningless place
The pain of the meaningless
gives rise to the I
to the I am
still meaningless
but this I
which rises from the meaningless
is the spirit
it's only the spirit that finds meaning
the spirit is meaning

Ezra said he wants to travel
the full span of his pain
because these sorrows
are the wings of love

It's where we meet each other
pain is the teacher

So I said
if pain is the teacher
then all my mistakes going free
Ee says his default state was loneliness
till he learned to love
Now no one's too busy for me
The moment we stop needing
we realize that that need was the pain

Pain? No meaning
but without pain
no meaning

Pain sets time free to fly
There is no meeting without Goodbye

They tell us life is compromise
Life is not a compromise!
Life is the event of the day

And we die
so that the event can grow into a myth
So each story has its ending
Our task
is to be happy in the end

Ezra pointed to the street
said this is the teacher
This is a great teacher

And the question
the question
wakens us from these dreams

And the question is
where will my pain take me?

past fear

ashes
(everyone is afraid of letting go of the holocaust
: for Ezra's mother)

ten thousand tears
haven't cooled the phoenix
she's still smoldering
beating her wings
fearing to remember
trying to believe the sky

untitled: "She's walking..."

She's walking the beach
arranging garbage
in meaningful patterns

Here, take this shell
No, put it over there

There's a bottle top
and a piece of string

Will she tie her mind together
or bottle her emotions
or sail away in a seashell boat
and see how far she can float

stark

I.

this stark knowing
even in fear
even here
this stark knowing
the spark of all things
being
a blessing and a curse

II.

Marko was sitting in the sun in the restaurant window saying that the
sun was the origin of all life, but I amended *"of all the energy"* I said
:but not of the information," thinking that the patterning comes from
history and happenstance (quantum and darwin). I was saying that
the sun's energy is crude. Marko thought it was quite fine, that it
spoke at least of origins and atoms and…

now why did that take me back to that *stark knowing even in fear*
and Tee saying *"the stark knowing is without love* and *love softens"*
and I finally had an inkling of why the wise have said that *there is
love and there is fear* and then my analyticals went
approach/avoidance pleasure/pain and I was on my own again

Brenda Poems

losing you

oh

losing you

was Jesus on the cross

was my best friend

so ucking brief

such a short I-love-you

oh

Searchlights Wrack the Valley of Jordan

There are times
when our fates
are in flow,
myriad patterns merging;
and moments when they lock.
Doors closing.

I remember the day
the last little phase
jammed together:
three years under the bridge.
We drove into the winter city
to tie in with the Joneses.
Tires sing
through the slush
carzooming down the four-o-one.
At the restaurant
my wife and Mr. Jones babbled
but I didn't speak,
barely glanced at Mrs. Jones.

We drove into the winter city
carzooming down the four-o-one:
a rabbit crossing the highway,
halfway across, caught
in our headlights,
stopped and turns back
into our path.

History's splintered,
a million pieces,
a legion of barbarians
stalking us with yellow eyes;
all our mistakes,
lack of faith,
the easy ways in and out,
little murders.

Catastrophe is stalking us.

Did you see the headlines?
the freedom fighters
have cut off the minister's head,
and troops line all the public buildings.

And now my wife is leaving
leading my children away
with her black widowed gaiety
rattinkling like shivering glass.

I know it's late. It's very late.
But should you find the heart,
the words,
to change the world:

cry loud banners,
cry headlines.

the rabbit's caught in the headlights
and the future's deciding on us.

Virgo Through Scorpio

was real but now it's gone
another summer and another time

In other cloisters time put on a veil
and walking slow and pale
beneath behind beside the moon
cast shadows and cast spells

In the lacunae between events
deep holes the void lie stagnant
Into these we cast our hopes and fears
as though we cast a ribbon
and a snake emerges
twined about our quarry
on the far side of the moon
on the far side of the room
fate is twined by wishes
and by the timeless I

Oh it will be so cruel
when you cast me away
you might take weeks
to get round to telling me
while vipers wreathe our bed
you'll veil your eyes
and move your heart
will I see still illusions on the shell
and sitting close beside you
whisper no-one's name

You see the moon
has blossomed snow petals
on a cream lake
Tomorrow's fancy
was my special child -
spoilt and unreal
it cries the moon back into place

pulls forth the full bloom

Ah, what-could-be I love you
already she has sung me
back to fragrance

Hear the crystals
now tintagelling
Guinevere's vacillation
See she moves her feet
her hips clasp that
mouth which dances
but I have no clue
how to receive the grail

which was real
and now is gone

another summer
another time

On Account Of Worry

because my head is bowed I circle
where are the doors in the carpeted ground?
and I think and I think what hems me in
because my head is bowed

> *this poem doesn't quite work*
> *hasn't worked through all its forty years*
> *for instance: the carpet is sand,*
> *the ground is the beach*
> *and the sea is a major theme.*
> *it's about worry, yes,*
> *but its about meeting the woman*
> *the perfect woman and*
> *and*

her eyes said you may look at me
her mouth said you can touch
her hair said you can set me free
her silence said ... .

you may love me

> *the poem continues grandiloquently how*

the wind drew my hair aside
to whisper the world is wild
the wind took my hair
shook it wild
to reach my ear

and say aloud
this child
this sister
see how she loves

because my head was bowed with worry
worrying the world
to tell me why my head was bowed
the wind called long before I heard
to raise my head
and see the sea spread wide
and far and furrowed.
full and wild
it brought me all I've ever craved
oh just beyond my grasp

that she even had a body surprised me
I was so lost in her face

back over the waters we flowed
I was the wind
and cuffing on the sea
sired then of her
the very waves which bore us

that worked better in the present tense

I am the wind
and cuffing on the sea
sire now on you
the very waves which bear us

and so our commotion
breaks upon the shore
where I still sometimes circle
head bowed
listening to the wind and waves
and wondering
if any of this has any meaning
beyond I loved you
through this fleeting storm
because the world is wild

Brenda

what a short moment
we'd crossed a stile
stopped
faced the wind
the future
I stood behind you
embraced you
a hand on your heart
a moment

the nearest I've been to home
the fleeting times with you
have flown
are foam

I trust we'll meet in heaven

No Downtown

There's no Downtown tonight
the clouds have snuffed it out
an interlude
gone
the city cleansed of all but nostalgia

there's no Downtown tonight
my melancholy baby's gone uptown
all the lights on Broadway
flickered and failed
and my consolation
is in a coffee cup

there's no Downtown tonight
the bacon is not coming home
the moonlight's been rented out
to the Rockerfellas

no Downtown
out of sight
sheathed by clouds
not a light

no Downtown
autumn mists
Downtown has been cancelled

The Bourgeois Blues

This concerns Lee Harper's amazing first poetic outpouring, which my father sent to Leonard Cohen. Lee was, and is, beautiful, so Ted enclosed a "head shot".

A few days later Ted said to me, "You write poetry," and the something like, "Wow! Your good. You're really good", and he sent my poetry to Leonard.

Leonard said he didn't think that I had transcended my bourgeois upbringing. He also pointed out that Ted hadn't send my "head shot".

So I wrote Leonard "a bourgeois blues".

The bourgeois blues have spread
way beyond Vienna.
Yesterday they rolled
under my bedroom door.
They crept up my William Morris wallpaper,
down the velvet drapes;
they stained the sheets
and ate my gladiola.

Leonard thinks I'm bathed in it.
Leonard thinks he's free,
But I know we're swimming
through the Company's dross.
This ain't the Jordan
in which we've been tossed.
It's the vomit of ages.

Babylon is a large mother.

Yesterday the bourgeois blues
rolled under my door.
Today I'll wash the curtain,
and hope there ain't no more.

Ted read the poem to Leonard over the phone and Leonard said, "Read it again."

40

Tell Me Christmas

something happened   again and again
and each time
it was like
it could be the end

he said
he felt
that she
demeaned him
she certainly found
that he tore her apart
he'd do it
and she'd do it back
a tennis match
they ate each other

most days
were up and down
vistas
till out of reach
endless beaches
spread
from the morning
like eternities
and this or that
would happen
glad things
and bad things
and things indifferent
endless beach
till I'd stub my toe
on a rock
or on fate
clack
a sudden sound
of accident
everything's changed
and you can't

go back

for Christmas
daddy came in
dressed like Santa Claus
he ho ho hoed
and pulled a shotgun
from his Santa's sack
blam
the whole universe
exploding
he shot the fugging turkey
kabaff

what do you do
for an encore
after something like that?
well he doused
the Christmas tree
in kerosene
and burned down
the house

and I sit here
and wonder
what happened
to me

tell me Christmas
went away

Chunky's Poem

Sometimes I saw the moon shine down
her face reflected
the back off all her dreams
a laughing stream

But workmen came in hire of order
built a wall that walled her in
to channels that her great grand dame
scored out between adventures

Between the lines
her thoughts flew back to me
and what we were
behind the moon and dreams

And am I hard and wholesome
straight as lance and substance?
you know too I am stuff and nuisance
jester poor and putty
weeping lonesome spineless
but the voice behind inside
that says I am too
I am too your kiss caressed

And are you soft and lithesome distaff
soft sweet child
tumble-spill wedded
to your lifeline lynx the past and
future play and dreams and feeling just
like you and me

I don't know where your fears should lie
I dare not feel sure enough
to urge you to your madness
but waters rise where love is cast
and don't know where to run

Love's reply

The evening I raised my hand
Even to strike you,
Jessica jumping
And the coat-hangers slaughtered
As we raged,
In the wind down
You spoke of the time
I struck Karin:
My only explanation was
What was I to do?
She attacked me
With claws and fury
And I used minimum force to subdue;
To humiliate, you said.
So what was I to do?
You could have hugged her
Love would have replied.
But you didn't.
That's why her love died.

The Ice Cream Parlour

Contemplate the hot day seaside town
all these people squashed together
pigeons crowded on the beach
seagulls screech

Contemplate the urbanity
urbananity
of the concrete's cold embrace
on the tar pebble shore
there are more tins of Coke back at the store
that's twenty 'p'

'scuse me
I was lost for a moment
between the sky and the rat race

A Strut for Alice

1975 Brighton
Theatre project
a revue piece

Francis…
later Visa Versa of Poison Girls
and some University students
torturing a drama about the body
we would take The Body Show
to the Edinburgh fringe

The body
Vi said we had to be totally honest
or it wasn't worth the spit
I said   well er
I have a   sort of
prejudice   er   ah
I find fat a…
it was just the wrong time
Danny
Vi's 14 year old Punk son
was trash in the kitchen
and Gary, her lover
was I forget
so Vi wrote us all
a Kitchen Floor Stomp
where she was cleaning up
all trace of us
from off her kitchen floor

a few rehearsals later   winding down
Vi asks me   Pasha! what do you want to do?

I said I just want to strut
Vi said well get on up and strut!
I heard distain
and I couldn't
but I went home
and wrote A Strut For Alice

I'm a tower of passion
and a cauldron of wisdom and truth
I've been perceived
as a power quite smashing
'cause I'm so perfectly balanced
hard and smooth

and nobody fucks with Pasha
but that ain't because I'm uncouth
I ain't tread on your tail yet
sister don't hedge your bet
take a seat with your brothers
you ain't deified yet

Alice remember the Queen of Hearts
she was raving right through from the start
I know the tarts that she baked
were really hot cakes
but the knave who enjoyed those tarts
remember the liberties he gave

me babe I just wanna
be another sort of caterpillar
remembering what the dormouse said
feed your head Flower
or you ain't never gonna see
no butterflies

The Baby with the Bath Water

what I think is that
when you was born
you was pushed down
and out of a narrow passage

your skull bones was squished
and shifted like tectal plates
pin head you burst
neath your mother's tail

at first you were a scream
a face a mouth
and hunger
and mother was all

or that bottle

then you had another end
and consequence
cramps in the gut and bupps
and little squeezy tease'ems
tumbles
life was not all ups

and then there was mother
and the wide world
there was war
beyond the window
and rumours of war
there was love
and anger and aloneness
in this twentieth century history
tottering on the brink

I had an oral phase
from the first
and a phase I got into "agency"
with my face
from the first

to my mother
I discovered my hands
and played with them
a lot ever since

I had a stage
a step
of denial
and a lot of this was around gut
and bum
and learning to say no

and I had attachments
to mum

and there were hungers and fears
urges and drives
some of them built!
and your hy.drol.ical model
e.thol'ged them just fine

and there was terror
terror drives

there is all sorts of drives
dig?
both in and out of relationship

out?
skewed about
down into the unconscious belly

and then
there was
the return

God is a person

the One that is
is a person
and I am alive in It

Mathew claims
that the One is a person
which one?
the One that is that that it is
is a person
and all that there is
is in Him
of course
and all that there is
is His

note that all that isn't isn't
so we don't have to think about it
because its rather murky
it can be quirky
so let's just say that that's that

I is
that is the answer to this quiz
though just what it means ain't so obvious

you see we are all part of that being
that is All and everything
which is a person in the sense that
It's a being and a being
in this sense
is an "I"
is a self
is a person

there are some though who say that
God isn't in the creation
She simply created it
but it's just a hop skip and jump
between Kingdoms
particularly from God on down

that's why they say
She meets us halfway
She/He's reaching out to us

Buddy God

so who is this person?
Jesus? Krishna?
and is He going to sit down with us
and have a natter?
and does it matter?

cause you know
the Buddha was one with the cosmic mind
and he said leave all of this behind
there's bliss inside this heart of mine
and Grace is for the taking

PMA: Positive Mental Attitude

A Doggeral on a Dogma

There is a place for negative thinking.
It's not always false alarm.
There is a place for negative thinking
Just before they drop the bomb.

PMA brought us formaldehyde
To insulate our walls,
And it also brought us DDT
To zap all that creeps and crawls.

It''s a kind of negative thinking
That's used to stop a war.
And when it's windy and cold outside
Negativity shuts the door.

Furthermore, many things are neutral,
And we need both yes and no,
So if yes... yes gets you pregnant,
Remember who told you so.

PMA brought us thalidomide
To put us all to sleep,
So when I caution let's think twice,
Don't just say I'm a negative creep.

passing sonya's

sonya too is left behind
her fat father's to an early grave
mother weaves abstracts with some small talent
we all have some small talent
thank god the house is paid
sonya sings jazz
it sounds like one song to me
and the world's left sonya behind

ah here comes francine
of the street up the street
of the street and madness
will she remember her dream
of the brass buttons on my greatcoat
how they gleamed
no she looks right through me
and i too am left
alone
a sunny day here on the streets in bohemia
the city does not love its children
and sonya's left behind

past lives

November still fosters
sun and dandelions
ragged like this parkette
in which I ply my calisthenics
Tai Chi hone me

below
leading to the street
is a tunnel of air
I could get lost in there
just walk into infinity

on the high street
crazy Francoise greets me
nice to see you
always nice to see you
but I don't open
ship in the night
no cargo to exchange
still coping with the last
do you remember
do you remember she says
how you used to sell water
in the desert
and how
the brass buttons
on your coat
shone
in Prussia

and there it is
that tunnel opening again
to magic
and to madness

My Baby

when my baby was my baby
the world was new
the fish were all jumping
and the sky was blue
then time got rusty
my baby got bored
and now my baby
ain't my baby no more

... baby blue

he loved her to pieces
through his needs and his fear
through tedious moppings
of mindless spilt water
and tedious movies
and tedious words

she never rubbed his tummy
they never rolled in the hay
they're guarded dogs today
circling safely
hardly sniffing
already familiar
already estranged
through tedious movies
and tedious moping
a few tender moments
but no high heels

I don't remember joy
when I was a boy
but didn't the days run on

they trashed him as a baby
the crazies
alcoholic mother demeaning father,
a sadistic elder brother
embedded needles in his feet
when the family finished whooping him
the world whipped him too
and wasn't Mother Nature unkind
in public and private ways
pain ago-go

the the then the last years
Dee started to stutter

a clever man
as smart a soul as ever I've known
except unable to take care for himself
ah but that's not a poem
that's just a moan
and didn't the days run on

everywhere in my house
there are things Dee did for me
or gave me
so much I always miss a bunch
if I give the tour

so many people that Darrell touched
were touched quite deeply

I remember
after his last haul back from the coast
Buck raving waving
a giant umbrella
in the storming park
yelling at the sky
begging to die

later he complained
"my social worker
doesn't understand
the difference
between wanting to die
and suicide"

now he's gone
and I've tears for a friend
ah didn't the days run
run

Dear Watch Tower

Will sassy teens be redeemed
Along with soft-core sinners
Or only zealots be esteemed
Amongst Jehovah's winners

The way is narrow with hazards lined
And words matter a lot
So sassy teens will be consigned
Into the fiery pot

What Do We Now Think About Mother

What do we now think about mother?
Who was the horror in the night?
I'm twelve years old and the house is empty;
I'm very empty outside your dreams.
You'll come home or die in a car crash,
And I will dissolve slowly...
Build a world of you own;
What will it mean?
I'm very empty outside your dreams.

What do we now think about mother?
Who is an angel who shines on me
Like cup-cakes and "it's alright".
I'm six years old and full of fear,
Guilt bred in front of a mirror -
Confusion and fear.
You'll promise me love and ice cream,
Or yell at me for wanting
Love and ice cream.
Now I will build happy families.
I never find what I want.
Where am I going outside your dream?

I'm twenty-five and look at your dream;
Happy houses, respect, care and love:
But your dream would be thin,
Even if it weren't already broken.
A layer on paint on who's wall
Keeping out the damp.
I've felt the corruption,
The ants, the worms, the maggots,
Eating the body of your mother love
For so long,
For twenty-five years.
I'm very empty,
Mother.
You die in a car crash.

Untitled: We sat…

We sat in the donut.
What could be more Canadian than this Tim's?
But now I'm the old geezer.
Jenny's even older.
She's my "Mother Project".
My restitution for the years
I kept estranged from my mother.
(Don't take sides, kids!)

Jenny talks of Danzig in the thirties.
She was just a girl:
dark haired, dark eyed.
They told her blond sister
not to play with the Jew.
"They stole my little ruby ring
right off my finger."
"Who? The Polish kids?"
"German kids. It was a German city
before the Russians drove them away."

"I remember seeing Goebbels
walking down the street
with some officers and soldiers.
I was afraid they'd see me."

Here in the Tim Horton's
all that is so far away, yet near,
and should be significant,
but it's just another day in our waning lives.

"The loneliness, Jenny,
does one get used to it?"
"No, love.
The loneliness stays."

Thank you Lord for the Flowers

one down two to go
they say here in America

this morning's anxieties are the standard fare
nobody's calm out there 'cept the Valium kid
and Megaboss lounging on his pussyskin couch
with the bourbon belly blues
no thought of Chernobyl
the ill wind the slow obliteration down the drain
and I might never see your face again
slow obliteration now inevitable
though billed second feature to the final jerk-off
Armageddon geddon geddon

death's death's death's
always had the upper hand
even before Auschwitz
but seldom has leisure been so harried
art that was Sophocles art that was Shakespeare
now it's Sly Stallone rehearsing the final jerk-off

the traffic cops are trampling the lawns of sweet desire
in this century as in the last the kick-ass boys are boss
and piety sobriety is just another jerk-off under the juggernauts
it doesn't feed babies
and we're just picking at the bone of all that promise

remember we thought love might endure
before Playboy drowned it in a sea of tit -
picking at the bone of desire - cankered prick -
to clear the way for tomorrow's big parade
Star wars promises a bigger bang
everybody gets a condominium
everybody who is anybody who isn't in the street
along with indifference

anxiety has gnawed at my stomach so long
I just don't care any more
I haven't the strength left for protest
that's last year's song blowing in the wind
the acid rain the cedars gone
and I might never see your face again
slow death slow down
come and sit here beside me
and watch the final jerk-off

I must confess I still believe in miracles
how else could we have come this far

two down one to go
hot house ozone winter effect
oil running out or spilling about
whales dying in the acid acid acid rain
dioxin food chain three mile Chernobyl

the more's the merrier they say
when three is not a crowd
more love more food more time more peace
more motor car The Chrysler The Ford
and The Holy General God bless America

I see
what?
I said I see that poetry is just another jerk-off
another peek in the narcissistic mirror
priapus
come again
I said acid acid acid rain
acid delusions wanking away
our one last chance to seize the times
seize the minds of one little generation gap
lost the time for one little positive push
one more try to be the good guys

hey, excuse me!
get off my fucking waterbed man!
these assholes think the world still owes them a living
the mortgage is due in Buenos Aires Johannesburg and Main Street
pay up punk!

three up three down cash in your chips
Ronnie Raygun has gone and hit the button
life's a bad dream
wake up in birdland
flash burning flesh pain despair game over.
will eternity trickle on in a lifeless world?

bang big fucking bang!
flash! finito end of story.
(sighs)

thank you Lord for the flowers
nice touch that

Pray for Israel

pray for Israel
she said

I in my politicals
said pray for Palestine

pray for Everyone
she said

Amen
we said

Amen

existence   being   is

the meaning of is
are
am

is is
are are
am "*asme*"
I "*aham*"
"*aham asme*"
I am

"*tat*" that
"*sat*" truth
isness
areness
amness

the meaning of am
being
I

I am
you are
It is

untitled: since all that there is …

since
all
that
there
is
is
I
am

optimize

Snowflakes

If each of us is different
how complex the world
all these snowflakes
melting

road-sweepers autumn morning song

the chill of the morning
tolls summer's knell
in this indian summer's
equinoctial doldrums
a morning of equality
in the vanishing days
my midsummer gone
maturity's coming on
autumn and winter's stark grandeurs
stands before me

this morning there is a nip in the air
but the clouds in the east are smiling
westward windward is clear and blue
and back in the morning sky
east towards you
the sun is breaking through
to warm my fingers
and promise a last summer's day

i sit above a calmly waxing
low tide morning sea
with my yellow rickshaw
road sweeper's barrow
its red spooked
sunburst wheels silent now
but soon I shall set off again
and send my barra's
squeaking to the morning

and this lazy sunkissed poem
i shall send to you

walking the dogs

walking the dogs
on such a gentle autumn day
before the storm
this beauty
in the valley
folding leaves and trees
yellow you know
orange
grey-green lichened sticks
all that stuff
your natural beauty
the light through this array
which leaves me cold
all these things are vanishing
like my drawing of Magoo
so fragile the drawing
just we two saw it
shared it
before I tried to embellish it
and the beauty died
like my several loves
that barely breathed

* * *

If life were long
I'd sit
but life is fleeting
so I run hither and yon
looking for a place to sit
and toast the days now gone
life flees right through us
folds its tent

* * *

I met Magoo the other day
such a frail face
bundled against the night
fragile as a robin's egg
already shattered
a lifetime ago Magoo dropped his first trip
not even a paisley he said
a lifetime on and he's no more filled
filled and empty
time has run roughshod through his face
and whether or not anything has happened
everything is done
a manuscript as long as time
bleeding its few memories
read once
now waiting a wind
to blow the covers shut
all my summers are gone
I figured one might come again
if I could just hold on

* * *

lucky leaped
he so enjoyed himself
dog bounding through the autumn field
while I worried the day

Fall Again: Walking the Dogs

don't I circle like the seasons
chasing my tail
or some tail
while there's only today
and it's rolling away

last fall walking the dogs
on this city park trail
brought me a poem
about frailty and ephemera

then I spent the winter and spring
hounding the same old things
and the summer chasing dreams

and here I am again
in September
writing
instead of looking
at the sun warm meadow
or listening to the brook warble   whisper
oh I can't find the word
and shoot
they've turned on the machines
clattering the world
clearing the bush

while Lucky dog bounds
wagging his tail
mousing
the seasons turn round me

turn me round
let me face
    enlightenment
there's not enough suck here
to sate me

and all I could do was scream

they went chasing into the bush
cornering something in the fen
barking
barking
and all I could do was scream
my voice breaking
time running
karma biting
and all I could do
was screech and holler
and of course they'd never come to that

so I ventured in
in towards the swamp
saw them hounding some
critter at the edge of the water
me yelling the while
too long and too loud

I went in through the rough
to the bog
thick mud
where now Lucky had most
of a muskrat's head in his mouth
while the beagle worried its ass
doing their best
to maimed and
and they'll kill it promptly
God willing
so for a while I didn't scream

Lucky shook the critter
but It hardly seemed to be dying
so I screamed
and pulled the dogs off
clumsily
they broke to harry the creature again
and I screamed them away

continued

it seemed alive
it on its rounded back
in the mud
looking at me
one eyed
the other muddied and
who knows
blind

I pulled the dogs off
covered in black
and left the muskrat
to its painful fate
painful dying
or painful living
cause all I could do
was scream

The Dugong Song

With the soft touch of a dugong,
With the gentle kiss of leech,
I am perfume of the onion,
As I nibble on my peach.

My lust for ripe pineapple
Cannot be concealed,
So I try my crab-like fingers
Never to reveal:

But I pinch and bite you
In the night, you
Know I have no choice;

And I'd try to charm you,
But I'd only harm you
With the grating of my voice:

So I'll put you back in the fruit bowl,
And go off on my animal way,
I'm a bit of a ravisher,
Much of a scavenger,
And I loved you yesterday.

the little red piece of glass

it either comes back
or it doesn't

I am an agenda
I write this piece
I mind the dogs

watching the wind
pulse through the grass
I can almost see the pixels

I close my eyes
my story still embraces me

it keeps coming back
or it doesn't
the little red piece of glass
or my foot
my right foot
as I sit beneath the tree
by the motherwort
things return
or they pass

I am an agenda
I write this piece
I mind the dogs

Watching the wind
pulse through the grass
on the hillside across the way
I almost see the pixels

I close my eyes and I'm still inside my story. Themes return like the
piece of red glass I found on the lake shore. I was looking for blue
glass or, hopefully, pink like Derek's art nouveau glass ashtray.
Derek owed me forty quid. We were both poor. He didn't pay so I
stole through his window and took his ashtray with its cool pink
glass lady. Then I lost it.

72

Thirty years later I'm looking among the pebbles for an echo of this mythic glass on Cherry Beach and I found a little piece of red: well, I walked past and registered a purpleness and went back two, three steps to find this polished shard of red glass and pocket it with the green and the blue, but when I got home it was gone.

Ah, the things I've lost: the small spherical Brighton beach stone that rattled, that's gone. And the loves, and a life,

The other day I had a flash, an insight into some underpinning of the world and went to for notebook and a pen, and it was gone, like the bit of glass. And though the next time I walked that shore I found two pieces of red glass - different thicknesses, different hues - the insight still eludes.

Back in the downtown quarry, I sat beneath a tree in the soon long grass, by motherwort weed, and worked at not to forget this verse. I rehearsed these words:
I am an agenda
I write this piece
I mind the dogs
watching the wind in the grass on the hillside I can almost see the pixels
I sit under a tree
the birds cackle overhead
I overlook a ditch where the muskrat corpse dries: the dogs slew it three weeks ago: they caught it out in the meadow, a few feet behind me, at dusk. The redwing blackbirds in the tree above me - does their "twee-wit" caution "dogs"? I lie back to watch the birds overhead in the tree. If I close my eyes I'm still in my story.
The beagle tugs. I sit up. My glasses. Where are my glasses! For three minutes they're gone, minutes of near panic. My glasses must be in hand's reach. "Beagle, damn you, sit!" The little red piece of glass, it either comes back, or it doesn't. The themes of our life are constantly in the woof. Three long minutes searching through the grass with eyes and fingers, and all along it was there just by my foot, my right foot. I sigh, and. I close my eyes. Will the river return?

continued...

Two days ago, across the quarry, on the hillside I sat with the dogs. A jogger came down the steep incline and Lucky barked. (Lucky is not the beagle. He's a cattledog.) I stood hastily. We all regarded one another. The jogger jogged on down the steep slope and Lucky went and nipped his heels. (He's a blue healer. That's what he does.) So now I'll watch the dogs more closely, as I should watch my mind.

At the end of that walk, an hour on, I looked for my glasses and found them gone. It was late and the light was fading. I'd look in the morning, and in the morning I walked right to them, my glasses. And the next day, beneath this tree, my three minutes bereft of them again. Grass stalks and stems, can they really blend so with the struts of my specs?

And two days further on, my birthday, walking the dogs to a new found secret meadow, for a moment I didn't mind my mind, and the beagle caught a scent and went, dragging us half a mile through bush and swamp, escarpments; Lucky bloodied in our crawl through fence.

Am I still in my story?
Sitting here beneath this tree
I watch the warp and weft
a web of themes
which vanish and return
like the glass
and the glasses.

I close my eyes.
I am an agenda.
These themes,
these things,
return or no,
and what sort of tree
will I find this to be
when I look it up
three days hence?

Untitled search for significance

Pattern is an opiate, an anodyne.
A wise man said, *Don't look for truth.*
Only cease to cherish opinions.

My friend Anthony
is chasing The All with numbers.
Sevens are magic,
Harmonic and limiting.
There are seven colours in the spectrum, he says...
That's arbitrary, I scream.
An indigo delusion.
Seven tones, says he...
Seven tones or twelve semitones
And don't the Indians have a five tone scale?
There are seven shells in the orbits of electrons.
I wonder if dogs howl in thirds and fifths.
Seven levels to the periodic table.
Somewhere in the seventh tier
Atomic possibility disappears
In an unclosed set...
But in black holes, I avow,
Anything is possible.
A billionth of a second is an eternity
In all that pressure.

Half a day away
Martya circles her ethnic origins.
Magyars rule.
I gave religion to the Babylonians.
I was Nimrod.
I gave Jehovah to the Jews.
Together we conquered the sky.

men again

Sheila said
it was men men men

I said it was tyrants
I conceded
we've an edge
on the course and the courts
in the bully's league
But Elizabeth rolled heads
Catherine walked them off a cliff
and they are just as dead
dead dead

But Sheila said again
it was men
and blamed us also
for repressive religions
it was men again it was men again

And though I argued it was tyrants
explaining how the Malay women
stayed in their native villages
and were strong with their brothers
even in Islam
it's not a simple gender thing.
It's control and property.
Spartacus rose against tyranny
and he writhed on his cross
for you and me

But Sheila said
it was men

fleet river

sit beside the mountain stream
and watch time
flow with the fleet river's lapping
ripple rapids spill foam on the bank
days flow by the same

listen to the water polishing pebbles
while the fleet river reaches
the surface of our dreams
time flows by the same

trees line the river bank
the sun spills through them
I walk in circles
days returning
fleet time changing
fleet river flowing
life flows on

politically incorrect
dark
taxi driver's song

black dog licks the water from the culvert

ugly housewives line Bathurst Street
I take them to their poker parties
and listen to them bicker
did you see the way she eats
behind each Zionist Attila lurks
but they tip like white men

dead kittens coat the road

untitled: what did Alejandro...

what did Alejandro say
I wasn't listening closely
something about connecting and belonging
flowing from a nurturing mother

but if mother is not nurturing I said
then ones default is need

there are ways he said
with a confidant smile

and the heavens gently shifted

Airport ruminations:
the Search for the Cosmic Fool.

Stuck in the airport, we stand before eternity. Only the chosen few get to throw their hats in the air. Mother has given me a biography of Coleridge. Coleridge is brooding with his ancient mariner. At school they drilled us with his monument. I'd rather be dancing with Mr. Miggymoo.

My son discovered Mr. Miggymoo among the Ibiza goldies. He's out there in club Mecca bopping with Miggymoo, dancing in the air, a spectacle for ravers. Oh he's swinging with the fireworks with his Shin Jin Rui crew while the whole damned ship of fools sails through oblivion. The whole pleasure cruise is dancing, dancing with Mr. Miggymoo.

Yesterday evening my mother and I looked through photo albums, one with pictures of grandchildren: many known loved images of my children and nieces, and some new images to love. At the front of the album is a picture of myself and Karin, my first wife. We are young and hopeful. Me, I was gorgeous, if cocky, a handsome winsome bastard - a happy hopeful lad.

At the end of the album is a picture of the whole family. Karin, post-accident, the two kids and I, sitting on a rock - a year before she kicked me out. Life had scoured us. My heartlessness, thoughtlessness came home to roost. No happy family. No happy after. My credit blown. Love flown. My nestlings scattered.

But here in the airport, boarding to cross oceans, I gag on chips and mayonnaise and second-hand smoke, and seal my grief again under the scurry of circumstance.

So here is a note for my daughter about how circumstance is king. The continents divide us. I horde your goodbye tears, and try to wring some gladness from my too timid soul and till I see you smiling with babies on your knee, I'll keep your love in my pocket.

And your brother, I see him dancing in the sky above a horde of clubbers, dancing with firework, dancing with Mr. Miggymoo.

Shit into Compost

The street I live on joins two main roads to the highway. It's never still. And yet we sit on a large, wild, well-wooded lot. The traffic swirls round our little slum bungalow. The traffic hums - it doesn't scream like at my downtown office - but there is not a minute's peace. What I wouldn't give for a moment's stillness and I catch just a moment's epiphany in the beagle's eye as the day spills by. The beagle's nose is dirty. She's been digging. We're tidying the back garden, raking through layers of refuse. I need to get the rake, and I try not to be afraid to go into the basement - the basement threatens to be full of shit of backed-up sewers.

Oh, I'm not a practical man, and that's a curse, but I'm cleaning up the basement. Cleaning up the shit.

Sue says she's learning to turn shit to compost.

The rake. The rakings of the lawn (less a bottle cap or two) are somewhere between good kindling and good mulch. Organic refuse. Beyond the fence the refuse grows thicker and more serious. The back of the lot spills down through trees and scrub to Mimico Creek and childhood. The dumping there is mile high: old tires, empty and half empty tins, bricks and bottles mid deer and fox and badger play - badgers in my imagination, which never stops producing rubbish, refuse. Garbage. The sandman is coming to take it all away. The sun is setting. The beagle's gone in doors, and the moment is still with crickets, bird call, squirrel leap, trees cloud sky...and traffic.

Obstinacy

we all seem
to be filled
with a certain obstinacy

in me
it just says no

in you it says
I don't believe

in the loud child
it spends its time
asking asking asking
nothing

fuck you
loud child

I tell you no

creed for the eighties

it's the greed of the poor
who always want more
that's why the world's such a mess
yes the world's starving masses
just sit on their arses
and that's why we're all under stress

if the unemployed would work
and not try to shirk
an involvement in productive labour
we'd all have what we need
and not have to plead with
our banker our friends or our neighbours

so go out get a job
and you'll soon be a knob
and wear tails and drive a Rolls Royce
poverty's just a pain
but as I think I've explained
it really is your own choice

new road kill

the joys and pain we take
from this kaleidoscope
are thin as gruel
thick as blood

there is a nightmare
on this beautiful glen road
wooded through the heart of the city
on this Friday night's drive home
two small orange figures on the road ahead
a fox visiting the corpse of its mate
I touch the brakes
behind me brakes squeal
the survivor scampers to the roadside

being near tears
I feel like a fraud
posing in my grief

this emptiness rends

so hush now

can you stop thinking while you breathe

qualify "kaleidoscope"
fragments
only fragments
splintered joy
thick blood pain
briefly here
gone again

Untitled: if we really…

if we really were God
and we had forever to think it through
in our infinite mind
then we would
and wouldn't
predestine creation

we'd surely throw the pieces
on the canvas like Pollock
let them fall as they may
so that quantum would shuffle
and Darwin would random fit
it all together

and the critters would of course
be selfish and relatively stupid
short sighted
and we'd be blighted
and blessed
with things just as they are

karin's hair-band

let the words flow
even if they capture nothing
let them go
release me

free I fly
through my eyes to...
stop
hold your breath
your mouth open
feel your sigh
the sunshine flickers through the window
it patterns white
and crowns with a light from everywhere
your hair
hush
not a whisper
only a silent sigh
moves in this wonder

your hair-band a crown
like a halo
not golden
like the angel's hair
that spills through it
green like the under-canopy of woods

see
we truly walk on water
only inches
from was
and will be

this blooming spring

death 's been courting me

I was walking down the road
minding
and plop a what
a dead pigeon
headless

(in the tree above
a hawk
a buzzard
winked)

* * *

I guess that was a harbinger for Crystal's call
I followed her into the Intensive Care Unit
a dream space here at St. Luke's
busy like a rush hour station
except for the patients
who are hanging on the wire
waiting to depart

a welter of beds and paraphernalia
a windy path through
where staff bustle   no
most sit at consoles
watch
or enter notes
oh I don't know how to describe
this hustle and waiting
this bustle and dying
all these separate beds
crowded stages
trickling dramas

Ryan is a stranger to me
Crystal whispers in his ear
Crystal calls
sobbing their baby's name to call him back

Ryan 's gone
gone over the moon
he's not coming back
and he's gone too soon

his hair is peppered long lank
salt and pepper
tubes are taped to his upper lip
but they don't obscure his face
an aquiline nose is slimmer
I never saw a more beautiful man
and there 's peace in him now
and that's bizarre
it's a substance that has tattered his brain
tearing him from his family
shooting the moon

Ryan was sober for twelve years
then binged
then checked himself in
and there
on the locked ward
fell into this

Crystal lifts his eye lid
nothing there
is that the mystic's void

* * *

how many weeks ago was it
that I put my dog in the ground
yeah death 's part of the landscape
this blooming spring

Hatred's Fount

I

I've been avoiding
that "other time and space"
despite a show of questing:

Those mountains
that we climbed,
and quiet rests
in groves with sparkling sunlight,
playing on this,
on that.

Every Sunday I've returned
to those hills and woods,
but now I walk
with a cold purpose,
a purpose that denies
the sunlight play...

Now even in those woods
I have a desk light
narrowed on small objects
that I've circled to exhaustion..
boring,
but secure.

II

Last night,
returning to the open place,
falling free again
from the narrow journey of purpose -
and opening wide
eyes and heart
in homage to last winter's trial
last winter's triumphal defeat...

Last winter I loved another:
  another world and master.

Last winter I was far from you,
  and so much closer.
Last winter I was given in sacrifice
  to this great pyre -
  my life;
  a burning wheel;
  a narrow fire.

I am ashamed of last winter,
  when I was minion of a petty daemon,
  creature of the narrow way,
  half light,
  spawned in the service of compulsion.

I am in shame
  and hold the leaf before my eyes -
Oh Father! I am naked.

Last winter
  I wanted needed
  my cold sister
  riding flame and billows -
  dark curling smoke in caverns -
  tortured tunnels -
  warm damp recess

III

Sister!
  black sister!
  ride forth:
  I am your chariot,
  I kiss the spur,
  and kiss the Gorgon's lair,
  the wiry hair
  its love hate and fear -
  the mouth of life
  approached in death -
  the pull of undercurrents.

on and on
and stop.

IV

Through the shame of last winter...
          its compulsion -
          the citadel
          of the white queen
          the black hair -
          our "*burning wall*",
          our "*falling tower,*
          and Agamemnon dead."

Again again
          assaulting
          the untakeable wall,
          the endless fall,
          scaling ladders,
   climbing past the peak-capped gargoyle:
          only to be pried from my crab clinging,
          tumbling from the wall

I prowled all winter around,
          about her pale skin,
          her dark mouth.

Falling,
          falling from the citadel.
Prick pushed,
          belly ripped -
          hers and mine.
Heart walled
          and open,

Eyes now blind.

V

Last winter a burning mire
          (and life and death) -

sin -
the devil driving -
whip lash
shit splash -
head screwed,
constricted,
pushing through the solid wall.

Riding to death,
for the freedom of the ride
the rip
The sword.
riding,
trampling,
onwards,
onwards,
forever,
death orgy,
forever,
plunging.

My great shame
of darkness
and of death:
The pact I signed
paying murder for the ride.

VI

What small parcel are we concealing?
just my childhood's dangling derringer?...
or perhaps a yawning, a hole...
another thought altogether...
worms.

VII

Behind me
an angel and lost child -
hid -
cried.

I cursed you too
        and rode you to the same mire:
My great shame.

        VIII

Last night,
        returning to last winter,

        I saw your face,
        and stumbling to the other place,

        your face,
        peeking out (the hopeful child),
        flickering smile reaching to me.

        decaying flesh and angel's.

I saw my soul
My hate
Your angel's face.

Winter's Words

Winter's words lie like snow
How cold how cruel my heart
Lies in its aching
Aches in its want
In the cold blind weather
And cushioning words I whisper
All's well
All's swell
Into an ogre
And organ growling
prowling beneath your citadel

Winter's boredom
A lie to lie in

First I free you
Then I tighten the rope
Strangle an image
Fixed form
Embodiment of my body want
Formless
No form no want
But wanton form
Ice melting into damp
Heat flaring into screaming
Leaving me unwarmed unmoved unchanged
Damp small fearful
But unquenched
With winter's wants
And winter's words
Set to begin the same again
Before the early dusk
Brings the same dark

The Crimson Rose

chased the crimson rose behind the barn
amid the mud and inch high foliage
rusted machinery left to dream
the silo gaunt looked on

chased the crimson rose behind the railway line
half cobbled streets
trees fractured
bare
but you are not there
nor at the factory gate

chased the crimson rose
behind the schoolyard
milk bottle tops
cast away wrappers
long gone chocolate bars devoured and divine

the crimson rose
the thread of your lips
and my long lost kiss

missed

what's up

what the up
are we chasing
over the moon

of course approval comfort
those things
and the ultimate thrill
enlight

sex them genes
live ease swhat's up
all them fancy free
and the devil's backlash

they are chasing hell down here
some of the sad
some of the glad angry devils
scouring our kids

that's what's up
going down!
that's what's up

Maybe Cynthia

(The "incident", for those who are privy, concerns Hyacinthus' underwear. Hyacinthus was a friend who Apollo accidently slew... so He made him into a flower. So here's a poem for Maybe Cynthia.)

We met with your pants down
and your guts blocked
strangled
starving
through mourning bleak hours
with and without the white flowers weeping
we found a way to unwind your anger
and your sorrow
save you from the surgeon gamble

hey
we shared such intimacies
all this is sacred

I'm glad we contrived
that I should never enter your house

in my house
in the heart of my sacred space
I have your "sample"
bottled clouds and innards
and beside it
I have your two faces
on the wall

so many layers

you said intensely
your said three times a week

the issues were:
what to let in
and what to let out

your inner doctor
a cartoon duck
said smoking was the big issue
that's grief in the lungs
grief in the lungs
choking you to death
my needles
just made them taste better

I said I have a problem
I find you attractive
I just love her
I could just
shit
I really think you're wonderful
you said
is that a problem
I mean
that's only natural
it isn't a problem
unless it's intense
is it intense
well it was intense
just at that moment
as I talked about it

but I never wanted
to get in your panties

I tried to make sure
you felt safe
that's why I spoke of my stuff
around placing my hands
in intimate places
bellies

there's stuff in bellies
and mouths

I told you I had Bertold Brecht's
four simultaneous mistresses
held before me as the ultra Byron
the beyond Bethune
or words to that effect
(well, were they?
(I said, tongue tied, simply
("My father was a fucker."

(My therapist points out that
(when we say something
(our words command an image,
(and that this image may attach to us,
(so be careful with your words.)
I said my father was a fucker
(I did not say that my head being
therefore sometimes cuntstruck/cockstruck)
I distrusted
the impulse to put my hands
on breast or belly
on intimate parts

in the sanctity
of my honouring you
you vomited up your secret
you felt safe
the pain receded

hugging would be too intimate

then doctor duck got weary
damp in the dripping
under your diaphragm
he suggested a vacuum cleaner
to suck it out
and my thoughts and my mouth
ran away with me

having blown spirits away
I fell into a contusion
of suck and blow

what was my grin
you probably didn't even notice
but wouldn't you like to know
I thought
of course you would
and why not
(emotional exhaustion
(my only excuse.
(my Naturopath says I "ebullated".)
the thought of sucking
below your diaphragm
it might give you hickies
I said
and yes that's an impropriety
bad fantasy
bad boy
said my notes to you
in my record of that last encounter
which you complained
was impersonal

it was
we had tried to jolly the duck
a dumb idea

hey don't I get a hearing
isn't there a "Herb"
on my side team

one bad day
and you're out
no second chance

continued

did I betray your trust
I was certainly clumsy
Cynthia walks away
and I can but hope she now has my gift
the resources to heal herself

but she who brought me Cynthia
is building walls
she's sets her heart against me
raging like her mother
digging pits
how's she gonna heal?

and all this is intimate
and sacred
and private
and hurts

untitled: I had this thought...

I had this thought
but it's gone
about the void and emptiness
'bout how life flows through us
like the bird on the wing
or the branch joining the tree
below the window
out of sight
this phantom is and isn'tness
the no thing inside
that we polish

**You Can't Smell The Stench
If Your Nose Is Blocked**

He fled from the bear
  into the belly of the beast.
Freedom! he cried,
  Freedom in Babylon!
In my backyard there are only flowers.

Friend, you don't want to know
  about the camps.
We'll all be damned,
  they're still burning.

Ivy's theatre

Graham exploded into the party.
Outrageous Darling
the inverse Dali, the tweed jodhpurs, breeches, whatever.
Eton outrageous.

Gray snubbed me.
Fuck.

Then Ivy entered.
She whirled upon us with a face and presence
like Miles' "Bitch's Brew".
She was outlandishly beautiful
or a weirdly funny black Diva princess.
She spun around the room with Graham.
They celebrated, outrageously.

Passing me on the way to the kitchen Ivy enthused,
"That Graham sure whirls fantastic!"
"I guess there are few," I said,
"who can share a stage with you."
She gave me a withering look.
"Do you live in fear?" she intoned.
"I do," I confessed.
She rose as before corruption,
rose to vanquish, as before the Devil,
them preacher's fingers rapping down.
"We hate fear!" she declaimed.
"We hate fear!"
Then she turned to consult Kim,
who was passing,
and came back confirmed:
"We hate fear."

Later we danced.
Later she circled;
circled zombie-like
looking for her gloves,
looking for her friend,
looking for the door,
Later she never answered my call.

untitled: of those dimensions

of those dimensions
with time its own
one and alone
and the pulsating strings
vibrating in
the three
manifest as space
spinning also through
six within
and then M-theory's membrane pores
yielding eleven more
dimensions
or is it sixteen doors
infinitesimal
and out there too
in the grand Oneness

is awareness *there*
consciousness
being
your "ground luminosity"
like the light at the bottom of the vineyard

damn
this doesn't convey the idea
that "string's" posited exotic interior places
and M-theory's further speculative spaces
track back inward will we meet the Absolute

is that where mind hides
just where we always thought
inside
inside inside

temper: the poem

my temperament and temper thrash

dan so glib
emotionless

i'd hex him
to a frog
if i could

he'd need that fairy kiss
would try to guile us
but there's no fairy kiss from me mate
kiss my chicken

and ribbit would just sit there
smirking
and ribbit would smile smug

where will beaupeep go when

Gretel spun out
    she knew she would
she'd played with the devil's pudding

what was she chasing
    or running from
    couldn't reach
    no easy chair
        collecting cats
Gretel
in her gingerbread house
waiting for glue or a patch

then she'll waddle   where
oh where will beaupeep go   when

no closure

Puppy Love Poem
which was titled "*Where*"
but could be titled *defaulting silver kisses*
or *fuck me, she didn't like my company*

where

I just did what I thought she'd suggested we should do
I fell in love

where

after the first electric kisses
she sent me boat loads of promised *besos*
then loved me silly for awhile

grrunt   (no t teeth) "nghuagh"
mm mm
hghaugh!

I thought I'd found the friend
but she said
not quite

so its nice to flirt
and tussle
but the smell of her was of home

besos des.a.pare.cido babe
kisses
disappeared   kisses

yes its nice to flirt and wrestle
but the scent of her was of home

where

besos desaparecido
kisses disappeared

lost and found:
intentions, agendas,
(unconscious mental formations)...

late Sunday
wandering towards bed
into the kitchen

on the table
a bottle
minds me I've a glass

wander back to the front room
and there I do not remember
what I'm looking for

until my eyes alight on it

someone called them hunting sets
of gulls
long ago
the sixties
when I studied such

did you stumble on the mind

Wikisays Nirvana Nibbana...

wikisays: *Nirvana / Nibbana* literally means
"blown out" like a candle

ni   out, without, away from
va   blow, as a wind; or waft as an odor
na   not, never, nor

van desire, love, win, possess, conquer,
        grasp, clench
van tree, thicket, quantity, wood
and *va* can mean weave
gatê gatê   gone gone

Nirvana Nibbana
wikisays: *Nirvana / Nibbana* means blown away
like a candle's flame

ni   out, without, away from
va   blow, as a wind; waft odor
na   not, never, nor

van desire, love, grasp,
van tree, thicket, quantity, wood
and *va* can mean weave

gatê gatê   paragatê   parasamgatê   bodhi swaha

Nirvana Nibbana
wikisays: it's literally "blown out"
like a candle

ni   out, without, away
va   blow, as a wind
na   not, never, nor

van desire, love, win, gain, procure, conquer, possess,
      grasp, clench
van tree, thicket, quantity, wood
va   weave

gatê gatê   gone

beagle burning

the beagle comes

the beagle goes

dry cedar leaf

burning

Come Clouds

come clouds
now that we are ready
eclipse our too planned joy
tomorrow we will plan again
today's already gone
along with childhood
back into the vaults of
would be...
might...
and when...

grey clouds
blue clouds
peach sky
willow tree and rain
tomorrow we will plan again.

do visit

www.normanallan.com

43019448R10067

Made in the USA
Charleston, SC
12 June 2015